THE THREE JOVIAL HUNTSMEN

IT'S of three jovial huntsmen, and a hunting they did go;
   They hunted and they hollered and they blew their horns also.

Grolier Educational Corporation

And one said ''Mind your horn and keep your noses in the breeze,

And then by scent or sight we'll light on something we can seize."

They hunted and they hollered, and the first thing they did find
Was a tattered scarecrow, but they left it far behind.
One said it was a scarecrow and another he said "Nay
It's just a gentle farmer that has gone and lost his way."

They hunted and they hollered and the next thing they did find
Was a grunting, grinding grindlestone and that they left behind.
One said it was a grindlestone and another he said ''Nay
It's nought but an old fossil cheese that some farmer's rolled away.''

They hunted and they hollered and the next thing they did find
Was a bull-calf in a pen-fold and that they left behind.
One said it was a bull-calf and another he said "Nay
It's just a painted donkey that has never learnt to bray."

They hunted and they hollered and the next thing they did find
Were five bonny children and these they left behind.
One said that they were children but another he said "Nay
They're nought but little angels, so we'll leave them here to pray."

18

They hunted and they hollered and the next thing they did find
Were two young lovers in a lane and these they left behind.
One said that they were lovers but another he said ''Nay
They are poor wandering orphans—come let us go away.''

They hunted and they hollered and the next thing they did find
Was a big fat pig a-smiling and that too they left behind.
One said it was a fat pig but another he said "Nay
It's just a London Alderman whose clothes are stole away."

So they hunted and they hollered till the setting of the sun
But they'd nought to bring away at last when hunting day was done.
Then one unto the other said "This hunting does not pay
But we bounced and up and downed a bit and had a rattling day."

Distributed under exclusive License in North America by Grolier
Educational Corporation.

ISBN 0-7172-9026-3

Printed in Portugal

E
C

Caldecott, Randolph
The three jovial huntsmen

DATE DUE			
APR 1 OCT 2 6			
OCT 1 6 JAN 0 2	1 4		
JAN 1 6			
MAR 0			
MAR 2 0			
OCT 6			
SEP 2 9			
DEC 1 4			
OCT 10			